Cadence

Life's Poetic Rhythms

Anthology of Poetry

Cadence-Life's Poetic Rhythms

Inquiries may be addressed to admin@prolificpulse.com

ISBN Paperback 978-1-962374-90-3

ISBN EBook 978-1-962374-22-4

Published June 2024 by Prolific Pulse Press LLC, Raleigh NC USA

Welcome to Cadence

We take pride in showcasing these exceptional poems crafted by devoted poets.

When we issued the call for submissions, we encouraged writers to contemplate the following questions:

- What do you celebrate about life?
- Who do you celebrate and why?
- When do you feel most joyful?
- How do you define joy?
- Where do you find the most happiness?
- How does joyfulness feel to you?
- Why is it important to find joy?

The responses received were both abundant and significant. Now is the opportunity to delve into the works of these remarkable poets and experience their unique perspectives.

Thank you!

Lisa Tomey-Zonneveld & Zaneta Varnado Johns

Cadence Dedications

To Max & Thelma Tomey

Parents of Lisa Tomey-Zonneveld

May They Dance with the Stars

To the muted voices of long ago,

yesteryears and today:

Allow the cadence of our rhythmic voices to awaken your joyfulness. May your silence come to an end and begin a new era where your voices resound far beyond the present. As they say in my birthplace, New Orleans, Louisiana, USA, *laisse bon temps rouler*, let the good times roll!

~Zaneta Varnado Johns~

Table of Contents

Inconsistencies regarding upper and lower case in names and titles are intentional, respecting the personal wishes of individual global contributors.

Sarfraz Ahmed

Uncoil Me

Uncoil me

Like a piece of spring
Breathe life into me
Let it begin
Take away the demons
The things that dwell
Hold me closely
Until I propel
Take flight
Uncoil me tonight.

Hooked

Not too shabby

You've got the swagger
The streetwise look
You've got me hooked
Completely in a trance
Mesmerised by the view
Now I can't take
My eyes off of you

You divert my eyes
Paralyse me
Push to the point of delusion
You create an illusion
That I can't let go of
Some call it lust
But I call it love.

Sunday in the Shed

Sitting in your shed

Listening to your vinyl's
Music pumping in my head
Relaxing beginning to let go
As we sat in socks
All in a row.

While we listened to the music
Talked about poetry and stuff
While we spent the time
Drifting away
Talking about the rhyme.

With cushions and nick-nacks
Surrounding us
Paraphernalia from yesteryear
As we drank and cheered
I'm glad that I was here
Letting the music
Drift us away
On this hot summer's day

It's just another
Summer's afternoon
Sat with my friend
Wishing the good times
Would never end.

Sarfraz Ahmed is a world acknowledged writer, an amazon bestseller who achieved success globally as a poet. His published books include poetry debut *Eighty-Four Pins - Poetry Collection* (June 2020, 2022) and *My Teachers an Alien!* (November 2020). *Two Hearts - A Journey into Heartfelt Poetry* (February 2021) with Annette Tarpley and *Stab the Pomegranate - Collective Poetry* (August 2021). *The second edition of Eighty-Four Pins - Poetry Collection* was published in February 2022, followed by the global release of *The Gift of Poetry* (June 2022) specially dedicated to all his supporters. In April 2023 he published *The Ramblings of a Romantic Poet*, a collection inspired by writers in the USA and dedicated to US poet Elliot M. Rubin.

Rita Anderson

Snow Angel

Toddling out of bed and out the door
before breakfast
on the first snowfall,
his.

Prints in the snow promise
wet pants, blue fingers,
red cheeks, and frozen
ears.

I cook and watch him
out the window, as he molds
the low row of an abandoned igloo,
the plastic sled swooshing
past.

"Will you come and play?"
Yes, I say. *Later*. His laughter
bouncing off of
bricks.

Us in one image (**Mom**: Milk, splashing in the pan,
burns on the coils.
Son: Sweaty appetite under knit cap.)

Watching him discover, I am
loved but outgrown
like his handprint
on a mirror.

Rita Anderson is an internationally published and an award-winning writer with an MFA Poetry and an MA Playwriting. She was Poetry Editor of *Ellipsis* (University of New Orleans) and Senior Poetry Editor at Red Dashboard Press (Princeton). Her poetry books, *The Entropy of Rocketman* (Finishing Line Press), and *Watched Pots (A Lovesong to Motherhood)*, were nominated for the Pushcart Prize. Contact Rita at her website: www.rita-anderson.com

Nanci Arvizu

A Song

Often there is a whisper of a rhythm
that pulls at the strings of my heart

a pulse, a beat, a thumping
coming from somewhere in the stars

before the words have started
I know them in my soul

written to grab my emotions
and make me feel the song

it might make me laugh
or it might make me cry

it makes me stop everything
it might change my life.

A song can leave me longing
with a memory of love

or make me dance and shout
in gratitude to all that is above

grateful for the songs
connecting me to my past

help me to remember
how grand has been this path.

In the Stars

Where did you go
What is the view like
Between Venus and Mars

Are the lyrics I wrote in the song

I wrote about you
after you went away
your forever adventure

some call it a grave

but I know you're out there

I can feel you on nights
when the sky is clear
and I walk in the moonlight

I see you between the planets
flying through the stars

and I know
you're not that far

I can see you when
I'm brave enough to look
through the hole you left
in my heart

Work by Nanci Arvizu has appeared in *Dear Heart* (essay, 2023), *A Safe and Brave Space V2* (poetry, 2022) *Social Justice Inks*, (poetry, 2022), *Fine Lines Journal*, (essay, 2022), *Caring for Souls* (essay, 2022), *A Safe and Brave Space V1* (poetry, 2021), Tucson Mystery Writers, Special Mention (fiction, 2021). *www.nanciwrites.com*

Bartholomew Barker

Our Smoldering Fire

Orange flickers of flame skip off your skin
and shadows play along the wall.
We tell the frustrations of our days,
the wins and losses, the melody of life.

Warmth pours from the hearth as we cling together
near crackling logs this winter night.
No fur rug— we're not that trite— just a blanket
already worn from years of living.

We don't need a fireplace to stay comfortable
in this efficient twenty-first century home.
The heat pump and insulation keep the cold at bay

but we still have desires—
a bottle of wine, a soothing fire
and each other at the end of the day.

Thanksgiving Table

We build upon a base—
first an autumn tablecloth,
a harvest runner, place-mats,
dishes and finally food:
turkey, dressing and pie,
and we celebrate—
mostly the stories
steeped in the wood.

Playing tug o' war
over a fragile bone—
giving flight to a wish.
Spilling gravy
on expensive lace.
Sitting on telephone books
beside the grown-ups—
feeling all grown up.

But there are deeper
memories ingrained
from generations passed—
Christmases and Easters,
birthdays and wakes,
wars and peace,
arguments and grace,
all remembered in the oak.

These kids don't know they're in love yet

and they don't want to be called kids
but from my perspective,
sitting as close to death
as they are from birth,
it's obvious they're in love,
the terrible kind that's forever.

They're too scared to touch
but soon they'll cling
to each other like wet clothes,
discovering the joys adults
take for granted until lost.

I can't tell who'll take the risk,
succumbing to the fresh chemicals
flooding their adolescent brains
and say the first "I love you"
nor can I tell who'll betray,
grow bored or get a better offer,
breaking their first heart.

But I smile as I watch
their clumsy courtship
and hope they enjoy forever
for as long as it lasts.

Bartholomew Barker works with Living Poetry, a collection of poets in North Carolina. He has published a full-length collection, a chapbook and been nominated for the Pushcart Prize. His work has recently appeared in Panoply, Free Verse Revolution, the Gyroscope Review, Naugatuck River Review, among others. www.bartbarkerpoet.com

arlene s bice

Fingers and Ears

Early days
Clack, clack, clack-clack
Clack, clack, clack-clack
sounds of typing class
rhythms of learning
I giggled at the cadence
so long ago
a memory of it brings
smiles of joy and laughter
gleeful reaction.

Computers came
Finger movement silent
Finger movement silent
too quiet, too quiet
sounds, I need sounds
engineers to the rescue
Click, click, clickety-click
Click, click, clickety-click
ahhh, ahhh, ahhh
sounds of contentment.

About *Turning Centuries* by Youngblood

Wumpata, wumpata, wumpata
chanting
over, over, and over
as bicycle wheels
turn, turn, and turn
climbing the Rocky Mountains
a lonesome rider
on a solo bicycle journey.

a Taos Pueblo Healing Chant
wumpata, wumpata, wumpata
found in a discarded book
free, on a small library step
beats rhythm through my mind
as I read of one man's journey
discovering life and healing
upfront and intensely personal.

Rhythm of Life

As water flows from calm,
peaceful pond
trickles out to see the world
builds currents
moves fast
around, over rocks
approaches boulders
drops down, down, down
as a waterfall
splashing back up
soaking all it touches
to settle again
a brief spell
eddies, whirls,
carries autumn leaves
dropped
from overhanging trees
full of color
my life rhythms.

arlene s bice is the recipient of the Florence Poets Society Poet of Distinction Award and the Annual Literary Oakley Hall Award. Her poetry books are *Simply Put* and *The Afternoon Crowd.* She is also published in several anthologies. She presently lives in Farmville, Virginia.

A. C. Blake

Chorus of the Young

In laughter's echo, in playful cheer,
Where innocence and wonder meet,
The joyful chorus rings so clear,
In every dancing, tiny feet.

Amidst the meadows, under open skies,
In children's eyes, the world anew,
Each moment a surprise, a cherished prize,
A view so pure, so bright, so true.

They teach us how to see the light,
In simple things, in nature's play,
To find the joy in day and night,
In every ordinary, extraordinary day.

Let us learn from these young hearts,
To live with wonder, love, and glee,
For in their songs, true wisdom starts,
The key to living joyfully.

Canvas of Creation

In the quiet hours of dawn's first light,
Where thoughts and colors softly blend,
The artist finds her purest delight,
In creation's dance that never ends.

With pencils poised and stories spun,
Each stroke a tribute to joy's embrace,
In worlds imagined, under rising sun,
She finds her peace, her sacred space.

Here, in the sanctuary of her mind,
Where dreams are painted, bold and bright,
A tapestry of life, uniquely designed,
Unfurls in hues of day and night.

For in each line, in every shade,
Lies the essence of a life well-lived,
A celebration of the art she's made,
A gift of love, forever to give.

The Explorer's Heart

In lands afar where wild winds sing,
'Neath starlit skies and eagle's wing,
The explorer's heart finds its tune,
Dancing with the sun and moon.

Through verdant forests, over peaks,
In whispered tales the spirit speaks,
Of adventure's call, so bold and free,
A symphony of land and sea.

This heart that beats in nature's hand,
Finds joy in every grain of sand,
In every leaf, in every stone,
A world of wonder, yet unknown.

So let us roam where dreams take flight,
In day's embrace, through starry night,
For life's a journey, vast and wide,
With the explorer's heart as guide.

Anne Catharine Blake is a freelance author and illustrator, her unique heritage, a blend of Canadian and Southern American influences, colors her works with humor and cultural depth. Internationally acclaimed, Ms. Blake's art and stories have been published and exhibited globally. Her recent works include contributions to "Remembering Sylvia Plath, Anthology, Moonstone Press 2023" and "Katherine Mansfield 100" video Anthology, Art Infinity Press, NZ, 2024. Her papers are part of the collection at the de Grummond Children's Literature Collection at the University of Southern Mississippi.

Susi Bocks

My Loves

lucky are those who've captured
human manifestations of sunrays
family who are friends
and friends who are family
those who light us up from the inside
and continue to dose us as needed

they sustain us
when the real sun
chooses to hide
behind cloudy days

they lighten our worries
when our own energy is depleted
and they add such value
all of the times

just with their energy
that is always permitted
and encouraged to be in our vicinity

these rays of love
make living enjoyable
and endurable

Profound Interactions

happiness and joy feels light
yet the intensity sears deeply
with events and people
bringing out the best in us

rare and fleeting
are those moments we cherish
wishing and hoping to hold tighter
the memories they become

we reflect
and we ache for those times
again and again

Freedom, Peace, and Harmony

being in nature
supplies a joy
unknown
in the day to day
there's no escaping
feeling it solidly
down to
and in my bones
lazily clear-eyed and soothed
i whisper back to it
good intentions
and many thanks for the healing

Susi Bocks (IWriteHer.com) has self-published two books - *Feeling Human* and *Every Day I Pause and was a Pushcart Prize Nominee in 2021.* She is the Editor of *The Short of It*, which has produced *The Sound of Brilliance* and *Reflections & Revelations*. Bocks has works published in numerous anthologies.

Yasmin S Brown

Life's Melodies

A song just for you,
Continuously playing a sound,
Of inflection and tempo,
Combining the melody of beaten rhythms,

With blare attributed to a quivered impression,
A gliding bellow of learning and experience,
Swaying repeatedly through rough turbulence,
Sequencing a time and event,

Flowing up and down,
Touching all five senses; taste, smell, sight, sound, and touch,
stroking our emotional strings,
Protecting life's melody is not asking too much,

An escort of beautiful, expressed melodies,
Memorizing memories,
Accompanied by a pattern of possibilities,
Voicing a distinct sound of capabilities,

The melody of life is what changes me.

The Orchestra of Jazz

With the stroke of a natural key,
enhancement of enharmonic,
Each tickle creates a tune that relaxes me,
An iconic jazz sound,

A light touch of the cymbals,
tapping of sneer drums,
In unison like a rhythmic wave,
Swaying with a hum,

In tune with the plucked strings on a bass guitar,
Accompanied by the clarinet impacting the flow of the saxophone,
Smooth groove you set the tone,

Impacting history,
Collaborating melodies,
An instrument of instrumental music,
Encouraging a flow of futuristic melody,

Swinging notes from a violin,
Playing a flute with a polyrhythm trend,
Amplifying an acoustic flare,
Evolving over centuries on air,

Roots of Creole, blues, and ragtime the sounds of your vehicles influenced expressions over a lifetime.

A Rhythmic Tap

Clickety-clack, clickety-clack,
Tap, tap,
Went the patent leather shoes,
With speed and precision,

Sound and rhythm,
Tap, tap,
As silver cleats hit the stage,
Dancing with intention,

A combination of stomp tap,
Clickety-clack, clickety-clack,
Waving his arms,
Tapping on his tippy toes,

Tap, Tap,
Gregory Hines from my time,
Choreographing his choreography,
Clicking on the beat,

Interacting with the crowd,
Through the way he gets down,
Clickety-clack, clickety-clack,
An inspirational sound,

Tap, tap,
As the orchestra plays a sound,
To the quick movements of his feet,
Entertaining too many,

Applause of packed music halls,
Stump, stump,
Clickety-clack,
Tap, tap,

That's a curtain call.

Yasmin S Brown is a certified life coach and Guinness World Record participant. She developed her public speaking and leadership in Toastmasters becoming a Distinguished Toastmaster. Yasmin utilizes her personal and healthcare professional experience to advocate for women's mental health. Through innovation, she brings organizational health, communication, and trauma-informed awareness.

Lin Marshall Brummels

White Blooms, Bones, Cakes, and Trucks

I am white hair framing a pale face, baking
white cakes frosted with light buttercream .

Guy friend is an older white Ford long-box pickup
pulling a stump grinder to clean up yards.

Son is a middling white one-ton pickup pulling
more than his weight in campers, trailers, and carts.

Plumber is a retired white double-cab truck, supplies
stashed in the back seat and in white metal boxes.

Windfarm repair guys are all new white pickups, driving
community to repair turbines, each in his own vehicle.

Day of the Dead celebrations feature dancers in white,
honoring the bleached bones of their ancestors.

Christmas cactus blooms white on Halloween,
two months early, joke on all of us.

Lin Marshall Brummels earned a BS from University of Nebraska and a MS from Syracuse University. Brummels has poems in *Poet Lore, San Pedro River Review, Concho River Review, Oakwood, Plainsong, Nebraska Life,* and others. Chapbooks, "Cottonwood Strong" and "Hard Times," 2016 Nebraska Book Award. Book, "*A Quilted Landscape.*"

Stephen W. Buchanan

For Well Being

There is no doubt
'Tis better to
let the joy out
so light comes through
than hold its kin
bitterness in
to spark the dark

Slippin' Into

Get up and do
Don't wait until
Days are too few
Make them fulfill
Time's unaware
Time doesn't care
what your plan's for

Spread Love and Fun

You get one life
so use it well
Don't foment strife
Don't create hell
Spread love and fun
for everyone
And be happy

Stephen W. Buchanan enjoys writing poetry whenever the muse strikes. He posts under the pen name Muttado1sb, which is a play on Shakespeare's "Much Ado About Nothing" and a mutt being a blend of many things because his poetry is a blend of many nothings.

Anupama Sham Budhrani

Joy is Found Everywhere

Joy is found everywhere
in little deeds, that tell you care
in helping the people, who are near to you
In doing routine acts and something new

Joy is found in people's smiles
Joy is found in emotional ties
Joy is found in a hi-fi
Joy is found in someone's sigh

Everyday day in little tasks you do
And as the day goes through
you find joy and grow
you forget all feelings of being low

With joy, life goes on smoothly
Joy is something very earthly
Joy heals a broken heart
Joy gives you a good start

So, never ignore the little joys of life
that come along the way, when you strive
Simple joys are a pleasure
They keep happening for sure!

Celebrations in Life

Every day is a celebration of its own kind
People do work and bind
The feeling of togetherness
The feeling of oneness

Celebration of occasions
Celebration in vacations
A party to go
Guests waiting at your door

Festivals to celebrate
Gifts to open, can't wait
Celebration is a happy state
so you don't have to be late

Celebrations bring smiles
laughter, love in people's lives
merriment and enjoyment
commitment and betterment

So, stop by and celebrate
a moment or two
with your loved ones
colleagues and friends too!

Importance of Joy

Joy is important in our daily lives
to express our feelings, that sometimes fly
To control all our emotions
Joy provides a good notion

Joy cures sadness
It maintains happiness
you forget all your frustrations
with little acts of joyfulness

Take time to feel the joy
Let it sink into your system
Many situations may crop up
of little joys that can't stop

Don't underestimate joy
it will fill any kind of void
emptiness and sorrow
Don't postpone joy until tomorrow

Joy brings well-being and health
It is a feeling of free wealth
It is in everyone's hand
To celebrate joy, you can always stand!

Anupama Sham Budhrani is a budding poet and author. She has completed her M.B.A and Post graduation in computer applications. She has been writing for 5 years. She loves writing. Her first book, *A Collection of Poems*, is now available. She hails from Visakhapatnam, India.

Nigel Byng

The Living Color of Youthful Dreams

Skipping stones on a first date, and doing a rain dance in a thunderstorm
Celebrating mere existence, taking for granted the moment things transform
Childish, whimsical, fearless, immortal
Eagerly anticipating the arrival of adulthood's portal
School days were happy days
Summer breaks a blissful haze
Youthful romance even then a complicated maze
But I'd trade you all of my cards just for a centerfold's gaze
Youth on the young wasted, never
In the moment, and in the memories forever a treasure
Exuberant like the plumage of a peacock.
Puff and strut, mamas' milk smooth, diamonds in the rough, untouched uncut
Best foot forward, failure not even a trailing shadow.
Today's unfinished adventure, the sequel has tomorrow.

Transitions and trepidations were an unlikely pair
Oh, we lived life never knowing fear
Valedictorian ambitions, mere wishful thinking
Just a class clown or perhaps a president in the making
How the hands of time changes with every moment
Nothing is set in stone, yet they're never out of alignment
What could have and should have is best left for hindsight
A wise man may think his afterthoughts before, but there's no fun in foresight.
We ran free like wild horses, just trying to live right
Youths dream best in living color, never in black and white.

A Summer to Remember

The last bell before summer, dragged on it seemed till November

I had my shoes filled with burning embers

A waning moon, bedtime too soon

But it's a small jump from the window of my room

Gone fishing, or gone missing

I'll be home before dark, if you listen, you'll hear me whistling

Teenage crush was only a summertime rush

It's all fun and games, everyone knows that boys never blush

Joy riding and free styling

Fully aware I'll return home to a hiding

You're only fifteen; what does that even mean?

It was only rated R no need to bust a spleen

I got a second piercing, perhaps too visible, it was only a nose ring

Not to worry, everyone else did the same thing.

No mom, you haven't lost me, it was only my virginity

No daddy, I didn't damn my soul for eternity.

I'm grounded? Unfair and unfounded

I wasn't even the one that got arrested

I broke my arm, the cast was like a lucky charm

Everyone eating out of the palm of my hands

One moonless, star shooting night to remember

Underneath the mango trees, a memory to savor

It definitely was a summer to remember.

Nigel Byng is a storyteller, and creative writer at heart. He recently contributed to Happiness in Unexpected Places; an anthology of stories compiled by global authors and media professionals. His articles can be found on Signs of the Times Australia; Hotel Masticadores, or on his personal blog at www.hytsdaily.com.

Joni Karen Caggiano

Sneaking Out

floral linens stretch, clasp with wooden clothes pins
dewy moss clings, rosy face sunrise, hymn by wrens
fish swim in youthful schools, whiffs of jasmine winds

calls of dancing chickens, lay brown eggshell
girls push on worn out swing, giggle, fresh secrets to tell
break off ends of green beans, snap, toss in pail

sneak out window, with cousin late tonight
behold spellbinding moves, from fireflies dazzling light
lay on our bellies, countless stars, sky is white

love the same boy, lives just down dirt road
give ears to harmonic songs, sung by large tree toad
now rock, paper, scissors - our southern code

shy gentle lips, who's gonna kiss this gorgeous face
innocence of growing up, in such a lavish country place
love a boy I kiss at night, yearn for life's once slow pace

Mama's Biscuits

wrinkles squirm like snake on paper skin
making buttermilk biscuits, with rolling pin
feeling guilty for how you know you've been

apron tied she moves with care
watch with hope, flour dust in air
warm brown treats she will share

smiles, gospel tunes while we wait
kitchen smells like heaven's gate

sits down, talks, curls her hair
kisses my cheek, her skin so fair
dad home soon, now fear we share

store kisses like treasures, a smile and a wink
love to watch mama when she does not drink
no foul vomit mixes with her blood in sink

smiles, gospel tunes while we wait
kitchen smells like heaven's gate

Safe to Dream

linger, like the motionless hand of smell
veins that feed minuscule leafage uncoil
skinny legs race to chase spring's new tale

freedom from my pain a way to seek and fly
shimmy up new moss, on my friends the oaks
giants of my world, a tiny heart they fortify

speak your whispers in my ears
don't mind today if you see tears
your language softens all my fears
smell of alcohol now disappears

capful of wind brings clapping jade leaves
caterpillar with red hair wears ladybug scarf
tug up thick trunk, hold tight to your sleeves

day whizzes by as birds sing me to sleep
sun turns dreams into coffee ice-cream
hidden by cover, safe to rest in the deep

share your secrets my dear trees
sweet flowers will kiss tiny bees
tell me next year no one will tease
until then, hold tight, put me at ease

Joni Karen Caggiano is an internationally published author, poet, and photographer. A 2022 Pushcart Nominee for, "Old New is Not Old News," The Short of It Publishing, she has been recognized for several accomplishments. Her debut poetry book, "One Petal at a Time" was released in June 2024 by Prolific Pulse Press LLC.

Theresa Carlie

Simple Pleasures

A steady patter is how it begins
A creeping susurrus
Filling the cracks in the evening hum
Gently, so gently, calling to us

Evening's rhythm slowly unspools
A familiar lull that's filled
With the quiet, constant tapping
Until all other sounds are stilled

We rest easy in the gloom
Hearing nothing but the storm
That sings along the metal roof
Whose coldness keeps us warm

As we hide under blankets
Reveling in heaven's tears
Drenching our cabin walls
Yet touching just our ears

Theresa Carlie is a soul mate, dog mom, and little sister. She lives in Austin, TX but travels as much as possible, especially in August, when the Texas heat melts everything. She shares travel inspiration with fellow wanderers on her blog, HeyTraveler.com.

Elizabeth Esguerra Castillo

The Alchemy of Life

Pilgrims in this journey called Life
Coming from One Source,
One Universe with swirling different worlds
Dancing, in a mass of Infinite Web
One fine day our souls will collide,
When our Higher Selves meet at the epicenter
We all long to follow the Light
The illustrious beauty that never fades,
Of the invisible thread that binds every little thing.
Each one of us is more than just an atom
Which suddenly appeared out of this cosmic journey,
Across the horizon, I see Angels preparing for a banquet
Waiting for our return to our One True Home
Do you want to chase the Light at the end of the tunnel?
Or would you want to go back to the life you once borrowed?
Spirits transcending into another realm,
No pain, no suffering but only eternal happiness remains
I see you smiling in the afterglow,
And it finally dawned on me, I am truly Home.

Elizabeth Esguerra Castillo is a Multi-awarded International Author, Poet, and Visual Artist from the Philippines. She has 2 published books: "Seasons of Emotions" and "Inner Reflections of the Muse" and a co-author to more than 200 international anthologies. Her works were already translated into 18 different languages.

Carla M. Cherry

Bahia

Sprig of rosemary in my palms.

The aroma of salt beckons.

I amble alongside coconut husks,

flitter of hummingbirds,

fans of banana leaves,

umbrellas of palm trees.

Strong current, the sign says. *Risk of drowning.*

Still, I take off my shoes.

Beyond the gate is the roar. Bronze sand.

Jade green waves of the Atlantic.

I am awash in seafoam.

Gasp at its cold, but plant my feet.

Soft hiss, as the water is drawn back towards the horizon.

The current's invitation to carry me many miles to my ancestral home

runs through my bones.

The sun rises suddenly like God Herself turned on a light.

Turquoise sky.

I grow warm with this solar kiss.

A shell washes up. Six shades of amber.

Turn it over searching for its occupant,

hoping this is a rescue.

It is empty.

A gift, one of my sisters says.

From Olokun?

Yemaya?

I wash it clean. Hold it tightly in my fist.

Lift my arms, smile at the sun,

bow at the waist,

grateful to fall asleep,

to arise,

to the crest and crash of wonder.

Flame

Dear Sallie and Joan,
My peace lilies, named for my Nana and my aunt.
Your slowly unfolding white flowers make me smile.

Stems sagged, apex of your leaves turned brown by sunburn,
our first few months together.

How thirsty you were, and must be, for your native soil-
rainforest canopy of Colombia. Venezuela.

It is why I water you every other day
in my New York City kitchen,
and thank you, in brook-soft tones, for cleaning the air.

Sorry for this whitish-gray, muted-blue-sky,
fewer days the Air Quality Index allows me to open windows
for us all to enjoy spring.

All the knowledge we possess, and still we
cut down trees for newspapers and books,
burn coal and oil to power our computers,
complain we are living the hottest of days,
that we have not extinguished Canadian wildfires-
often started by lightning
but would burn less fiercely if the land and trees
were not dried out by global warming.

What azure joy would sparkle against the sun
if we followed the lead
of your fragrant flora, our fellow fauna-
maximize sun and wind to fuel our food, work, and fun.

Carla M. Cherry is a high school English teacher. Her work has appeared in Random Sample

Review, Anti-Heroin Chic, 433, Raising Mothers. Her books Gnat Feathers and Butterfly Wings, Thirty Dollars and a Bowl of Soup, Honeysuckle Me, These Pearls Are Real, and Stardust and Skin are available via iiPublishing.

Lauren M. Clemmons

Time with You.

If JOY could Leap from this Page
What would JOY look like?
Time with YOU.
If JOY could Leap from this Page
What would JOY feel like?
Time with YOU.
If JOY could Leap from this Page,
What would JOY sound like?
Time with YOU.
If JOY could Leap from this Page,
What would JOY do?
Spend Time with YOU.
Walk with YOU. Talk with YOU.
Eat lunch with YOU.
Drink coffee with YOU.
Watch T.V. with YOU.

If JOY could Leap from this Page,
Then I could not Miss YOU.
JOY would be YOU!

Like I Said, She Ain't No Puritan!

Get lost Puritan! She's gonna'
Dance Disco, Funk with R&B and Jive her hips!
Out of the way Puritan! She's gonna'
Rock with You, Shake her Groove Thing, n' Get
down Tonight!
Step aside Puritan! She's gonna'
Get up, Get down, Get funky, Get loose,
Boogie Oogie, Oogie, Groove Tonight, n'
Celebrate Good Times,
c'mon!

Ain't no Stoppin' her now Puritan. She's on the
move!
She's gonna' Make that Move Right now, Whip it
good! Burn Rubber on me and be Burnin' Down
the House while She Busts a Move--Can't touch
This!
She's gonna' Take her Time to do it right,
'Cause if She can't have you, She don't want nobody
baby,
She feels for you, She thinks she loves you, She's
Upside Down,
The Second Time Around with her is better than
the first time,
Tell it to her heart, you make her dreams come
true,
She feels like Dancin'! She's gonna' dance the Night
Away!

It's got to be Real, Puritan!
Livin' it up, Friday Night,
In Funky Town to Rock Steady,
Shake You Down, Stomp, and oh,
What a Night! She will Survive and She won't
Stop 'til She gets enough,
'Cause these are the Good Times!
Ain't nobody does it better than her,
Makes those moves, makes her feel This Way!

Puritan, by now you must know.
She's the Dancin' Queen, feel her reign,
Joy to the World, all the boys and girls,
Walk this way, bounce, rock, skate, roll,
She's havin' the Time of Her Life
She will Rock You, She's Stayin' Alive!
Ain't no Puritan high enough, ain't no Puritan low
enough,
Ain't no Puritan wide enough,
To keep her away from Dancin'! To keep her away
from Fun!

The Measure of Joy in a Legal Career

We can measure a legal career
By Briefs and Oral Arguments, Wins and Losses;
Dedication to our Profession---
Too long into the Night, worn out bodies, worn out thoughts:
Ideas that once made sense, now bereft of any intelligence.

We can measure a legal career
By adherence to our own Performance Standards:
Thorough research; painstaking analysis;
The repeated editing of the written word; integrity in our work product;
The Zealous commitment to make things "right"; seeking Truth and shining Light.

We can measure a legal career another way:
The Trusted Confidante. The Listener.
Steadfast, loyal, honest, compassionate, empathetic.
Grounding and guiding through disappointment or confusion;
The Trusted Confidante's allegiance is no illusion.

How else can we measure a legal career?
After many years in this Profession, I believe
That the truest measure, which exists,
Is Friendship---Friendships built and maintained, the kind that persist.

Some things mark Time for the Moment: Wins and losses;
Work well-done; sound advice given; the best brief ever written.
But a Friendship sustained, like the sun that rises,
Marks Time for the Duration of the life that defines us.

Twenty-eight years ago a Friendship began:
Two lawyers; two briefcases; and Bunches of lunches!
Twenty-eight years later, without further delay on this joyous day:
For your Dedication to Our Friendship; For your Honesty and Dependability;
For your Loyalty; For Listening; For Accepting; For Making Time;
For your Unwavering Support;
My True Friend, Thank You
For being the Measure of Joy in my Legal Career!

Lauren Clemmons is a lawyer and published author based in Raleigh, North Carolina. Her essays, poetry, and fiction appear in anthologies, including TAF publications.

Ambika Devi

Mama 102

Row of Peonies
white wrought iron furniture
Memories of you

crusty bread, butter
glass of white wine filled laughter
rainbow on my heart

one hundred and two
flowing forever in me
your love eternal

Thought

Autosuggestion
change your thoughts, change the mind
manifest desires

take needed action
scoundrel becomes into saint
forgiveness of past

honor positive
giving gratitude daily
you are Divine source

flexible choices
mindful spontaneity
How will you invest?

Susan

Cattails remind me of you
listening to them play
tiny rhythms
recalling the armful's harvest
down at the pond

We soaked them in the tub
your dexterous digits
teaching me to twist them 'round
fragrant pine needles

The scent of fir trees
eases my darkness
when wintry winds
dare to snatch
the Sun from view

Ambika Devi is an international award-winning author of six books, an astrologer, a meditation Jedi, and creative sexagenarian who stuffs her backpack with colored pens, a journal, a kindle, a passport and a deck of tarot cards. Her newest book, *Cupid is a Bastard*, guides the reader to self-love.

AmbikaDevi.com

kapardeli eftichia

spring gentle rain

Through the thin shadow
the small cloud
a sudden peaceful, humble
spring gentle rain
irrigates the soil

From music and
frantic dance
the most
small forgotten
grass awakening
are delivered, thirstily

In this hugging the
full of smells
Sun lowers
smiling again winner
the calcined stones
the rain thousands of kisses
he had left

Horseman

Riding on my horse
with the pale moon
travel
human voices
lost

My country away
I hear the partition herb
to my gallop

From the vault of Heaven
the stars fall to earth
glowing with fire
And when the sun rises
the distant horizon birds
show me with white lines of light
of the road East

Untamed Nestlings

The red roofs
Caged light touch
the lids
the red stone
flourished hope
single fruit

The built martin
the nest there
in the same city
The new Spring
will bring

The thirst of love
under cover
blossoms will invite
with dewy

Water the roots
meet you Joined
on earth fissure
sharing
I'll show times

The stars slept
with prize
Heaven
apart to meet
again Sun
and left
without a way back

I Am Free

Seasons, lives, escapes
They overflow
Flags, victories, swords white
Chrysalis in fluid bodies
Fire dancers of light

The rose of a red heart
In love the innocent beauty hide

In the white garment of the Sun
And the kisses on the cheeks
Ah!! I am now free

About kapardeli eftichia: She has a degree as an art conservator 2021. She has a Doctorate from Arts And Culture World Academy. International Ambassador of the International Chamber of Writers and Artists LIC, Member of the World Poets' society and poetas del mundo, member of the IWA, member of Ε.Ε.Λ.Σ.Π.Η The Union of Greek Writers-Authors of the Five Continents, member of the International Society Of Greek Literatures-Artists-DEEL and PEL (the World Association of Writers in Greece) Panhellenic Union of Writers http://eftichiakapa.blogspot.gr/2013_10_01_archive.html

Richard Fireman

Heartbeat Hotel

I take my daily human measures:
        pulse, temperature, blood pressure
inscribed in a medical journal,
        chart to my past and future
Each tick of the clock breaks up the stream
        into instants, atoms of time,
all the beats merging into waves
        in which we swim our lives

New Year's Revelation

It is the last day of the year.
How strangely we mark time,
as though it could be measured.
As though the sun could be cut
into a million flames,
as though the times of love and loss
could be any more or less
than their instants
of ecstasy and grief,
could contain the pain
or explain kisses.

It's always later than you think

They say my heart stopped for six seconds

even though I didn't feel a thing

When I hear talk about another war

should I even care since I've lived my life?

Or is each moment now more precious

because so much less time is left?

Instead of being just like the last

each instant is like nothing ever

Each kiss, each twinkle of the sun, each smile

sets the newest world on fire

Richard Fireman, writing for over fifty years, has given readings at several libraries and Barnes & Noble, and has published over a hundred poems. In 2009 he contributed a chapter to the bibliotherapy book Writing Away the Demons.

His first poetry collection, Constellations, was published by Prolific Pulse Press in December 2022.

Nolcha Fox

Digger

Sorrow is a digger. She digs a hole inside of me. Sorrow plans to excavate past my heels and replace me with a parking structure and luxury hotel. She digs and digs. All she sees is dank blackness. She doesn't understand that she is only making room for the joy that follows in her shadow.

Errands

Wind snatched my list and sent it up,
I followed with my eyes
and saw the snow-capped mountains,
clouds wafting through blue skies.
If I could only shadow my errands up above,
I might not get my shopping done
but I might snatch tomorrow.

This very moment

holds me in her arms,
rocks me to moonbeams
on puddles,
whispers sweet daffodils,
covers me with clover,
until I fall asleep.

Nolcha Fox's poems have been curated in print and online journals. Her poetry books are available on Amazon and Dancing Girl Press. Nominee for 2023 Best of The Net, 2024 Best of the Net Anthology. Nominee for a 2023 Pushcart Prize. Editor for Chewers & Masticadores, Garden of Neuro.

Website: https://bit.ly/3bT9tYu
Facebook: https://www.facebook.com/nolcha.fox/
Twitter: https://twitter.com/FoxNolcha
Medium: @nolchafox_14571

Carol Coven Grannick

The Night the Opera Singer Did Broadway Show

Tunes

If you watched you would have seen
that sounds wanted to escape

from arthritic bodies of the salt-and-pepper-haired
who populated ballet classes in the fifties and sixties

and were the singers - maybe even soloists -
of high school choirs and village shows

now picnic-eaters with fingers tapping
and buttocks bouncing, sitting on blankets,

walkers and readers, widows and couples
and partners rich with lives distant

from one another but buzzing together
with this music, this music that boils joy

that pulls us into one group because
it's one thing we all have

that made us happy in sad times
delighted in happy ones.

We know all the words
want to sing along with the voice that fills open air

but instead we listen, pretend her voice is ours,
mouth the words or whisper-sing and smile

except for that one there, the woman
at the perimeter of the pavilion

in a many-colored culotte
and an orange sweater that might not match—

she swishes and sways,
kicks up her legs side to side,

busting loose for herself and the rest
of us cowards, dancing and dancing,

dancing and singing the words
out loud.

Sassy Spring Arrives With Music

On the dark barren prairie the burn has shorn clean
while the winter warms slightly and hints bits of green
the air hums with moisture and geese nibble grass
and my feet bounce in tune with the springtime's sweet
sass.

Falling in Love with Winter

Red light turns green,
then a slow curve left creates
a straight line into country.

The city-world unzips, gushes blue and white
into chest, then shoulders and arms
hands tingling on the wheel

naked trees stretch, embrace space
dance in abandon against the azure sky-curtain
their shapes revealed and adjusted by wind.

A smile creeps into pockets
of mouth-wrinkles filling citified face
with country-love, song of life's cycles

car whistling through winter
winding past frozen acres, fallow land,
corn stalks peeking through snow

stitching a quilt across winter
begging for equal love, equal attention
rather than being seen

only as the necessity for spring.

Carol Coven Grannick writes for adults and children, most recently published in *The Birmingham Arts Journal, Poetry NI+, Capsule Stories*, and others, and children's magazines *Cricket, Ladybug, Babybug, Highlights, Hello*, and *The Dirigible Balloon*. Her verse novel, REENI'S TURN, debuted in 2020.

Joel Haas

Your Eyes

Your eyes--
those bright gray wells--
I always loved first

your eyes.

I loved your skin, your hair,
your voice,
your lips which never slaked
kisses' thirst.

I loved your every secret place;
at dawn and spring,
at night and winter.
I loved you upon our satin sheets.

I have loved you fifty years.

Still,
every poem I write
is for
your eyes,

For,
I loved first,

your eyes.

Immured

Still
in my latter days
I see you
as I saw you
in our youth.

Your skin, smooth and white
as quartz polished eons
by a river's hand;

Your hair,
a waterfall of silk,
to splash upon the small of your back.

Your eyes and smile
lighting landscapes to brilliant noon.
And, your voice,
soft--
a brook in summer--
soothing, cooling
all whom it waters.

This is how I hold you
--immured--
in the high keep
of my castled memory,
where the dragon of my mind's eye
guards my treasure.

The Angel, Nature

The angel, Nature,
Cloaks the sky with night
To lie
hidden,
unseen,
showing her passion
by starlight.
And when
The angel, Nature,
Doffs her cloak of night,
She stands naked, transparent,
That we may see her beauty
By the light.

Joel Haas spent 40 years as a sculptor. He believes Michaelangelo was right—sculpture is about taking away until only the essential form and meaning remains. At 72, he found words easier to lift than stone and steel. Poetry is taking away words until only the essential message is left.

Mark Andrew Heathcote

Scarlet Robins

Wild meadow scent-
succinct from anything else.
One yard of silk...
The bridge stretches out.
The pier rests in no-man's land.
Salty-rains cadence.
They verbatim to
suggest winds are destructive,
storms-eye peaceful.
Chestnuts gathered
baked on a roasting tray
Scarlet Robins dart...

In celebration
Let's dance till the banquet-
of opals runs dry.

I still love your words

I still love your words, and now you have a voice-
that is bewitching - in its cadences.
You talk of cuckoos—birds—and my heart rejoices
You talk of vines and quiet awakenings.
And how your words claim a right to haunt
while I remember my inertia.
Ah, how my own words were given applause-
complementing each other and vice versa.
I still love your words, and how much have they
grown?
Your old cuckoo birds are now nightingales.
Your vine, morning glory, entwines a throne
Not one word would I edit or curtail.
You talk of cuckoos—birds—and my heart rejoices
Talk of vines now; aren't these my languages?

Mark Andrew Heathcote is an adult learning difficulties support worker. He has poems published in journals, magazines, and anthologies online and in print. He resides in the UK and is from Manchester. Mark is the author of "In Perpetuity" and "Back on Earth," two books of poems published by Creative Talents Unleashed.

Duane L. Herrmann

Giving Voice

Those who give voice
to the voiceless
gather to share
and delight
in success when
they achieve goals
of transformation
of lives and hearts
from darkness
to understanding
and acceptance
of new visions,
new possibilities
to broaden horisons
of those with no voice
and empower them
to dream and arise
to fulfill their lives.

Trials for Growth

Trials of life,
and pain,
hone a soul
to be free,
detached
from physicality,
to enable growth,
of the real kind,
and perspective
from tiny self
to magnanimous soul;
pain, pain, more pain,
is necessary
sometimes
for exaltation.
We should strive
to see the end
in the beginning.

To Fly Free

Broken cage
does not harm
the little bird,
but it is free.
Free to fly,
free to be
bird essence
that it is.
Do not attach
to the cage,
it will pass
and we will
each be free
to fly
as we truly
are to be.
To fly,
is our destiny.

Duane L. Herrmann has carried baby kittens in his mouth, pet snakes, and conversations with owls, but careful not to anger them! Published in print and online, with degrees in education and history, despite a traumatic, abusive childhood embellished with dyslexia, ADHD, now also: cyclothymia, situational mutism, an anxiety disorder and PTSD.

Chyrel J. Jackson

Nature's Symphony

My life's rhythm moves and
Is heard in many forms.
When I'm walking in fall's
early morning the rustle of
crackling, falling, leaves
greet me as they say hello.
The tiny birds fluttering
above in blue skies chirping
sweetly singing nearby.
Life's music sometimes
outside in my front yard
the love of humanity as
taught to me from parents
who loved and searched for
God.
Morning walk now ended.
I inhale contently and smile
serenely; nature is the most
joyful and melodic sound ever
heard first thing early morning.

Blackbird Simone

Confident, Courageous, Gifted.
Talented, Strong, Rebel.
Intelligent, Activism, Civil
and Women's rights.

Whenever Nina performed her people
Lifted.

Conscience, Nina Simone was WOKE long

before the word was ever birthed.
Nina set and determined a Black woman's
worth.
She referred to herself as a Rebel with
a cause.
Standing ovations performing in
Europe receiving White and Black applause.
No one caressed or delivered life and
breath to a lyric like Nina did.
Celebrating Black culture honoring
ethnicity.

She was Women's Lib.
I think about Nina and all that she
left behind proclaiming her greatness
today,

Nina Simone a woman to be remembered
for all of time.
A woman who lived an extraordinary life.
Nina Simone enchanted a nation here and abroad.
When Nina sang to us we felt the presence
of God.
Known to the rest of the world as Nina Simone but

but for my dad and I she will always be our little girl

blue.
Our divine Blackbird soaring in and beyond the sky;
a woman to be remembered for all of time.
When that distinct crackling of the needle meets vinyl;
I hear Nina's bluesy Contralto textures
& tones and I still experience the presence of
God.

Melancholy Bluegrass Melodies

During my mother's tears
her pain echoed from the
Negro Spirituals heard
playing in the background.

Kid birthday parties have
Mommy's house humming
the happy birthday song as
the stereo blares in celebration.

Family barbecues, holidays,
dinners, and every day in
between, our lives were filled
with dad's raucous blues.

Even in death and last goodbyes
I remember the love and music
my parents shared in their lifetime.
I shed my own tears now.
I remember my parents,
our lives, and I'm comforted
in their absence;
by their loving memories.

A split-level, two story Kent
Ranch house that sounded
melancholy bluegrass melodies
that cause a grieving heart to
revisit a tear-stained memory lane.

Chyrel J. Jackson is a Literary visionary and #1 Ranked Best Selling Amazon Author. Reared and raised in the South Suburbs outside Chicago. Chyrel now resides in Red Banks, MS.

Chyrel Jackson writes in the spirit of her past great Literary ancestors. 2021 garnered Chyrel her very first literary nomination, Pushcart Nominee-Poem Love Unspoken, Published in Heart Beats Anthology.

Chyrel has published Mirrored Images and *Different Sides of the Same Coin. She also appears in multiple published* poetry Anthologies. You will find Chyrel always writing.

You can find her on Sistersrocnrhyme.comhttps://linktr.ee/ChyrelJ_Jackson66

Gerald Jatzek

Tioman

The stone dragon's island:

In the morning the lizard narrowly

flicks his tongue into the salty air.

Blessed be the day, and the month, and the year:

If you stood at the window,

a unicorn would emerge from the jungle.

Crete, South Coast

We came by boat and entered
a cloud of languages. The room
we chose was not for rent.

We gathered stones and built
a wall: a home of sorts
under the salt cedar.

We took up residence. Cicadas
raised their wistful sounds
before the tide got high.

Gerald Jatzek is a poet and musician from Austria, who writes in German and English. He has published books and songs for children and adults. 2001 he won the Austrian State Prize for Children's Poetry. His poems have appeared in anthologies and literature papers in Europe, India and the USA.

Zaneta Varnado Johns

Love Unconditional

I sway harmoniously with
the people who know me
the people who reflect me
the people who cannot wait
to indulge me

My heart pulsates to the rhythm
of love unconditional
Intense magical enthusiasm
how sacred the sound
how sweet the taste
how warm the touch

I am truth
I lay bare the worst of myself
without conviction
My best self is
appreciated... illuminated... celebrated
with love and laughter

Consumed with gratitude
I trust with fortitude
I reside in a cloud of
God's amazing grace—
my happy place

Appreciation

For some, tomorrow did not come
I started my day with a happy hum
Stepping to the beat of my Savior's will
His heart's desire I must fulfill

The universe gives whatever I need
I avail myself to do good deeds
My wish for others is peace and joy
Kindness is my leading ploy

Nature's spectrum pleases my sight
Colorful habitats to my delight
My jubilant heart cannot deny
dazzling beams from earth to sky

Pleasure swirls deep within my soul
Relations bolster as I grow old
I value life lessons borne from strife
I treasure the gift of my favored life

Joyful Haiku Medley

Sunrise offers light

Path is illuminated

The way becomes clear

A listening ear

Warm bench with an empty seat

Hugs on arrival

Past filled with treasures

Engage mindfulness today

Tomorrow awaits

Rainfall and whispers

Connections to the divine

My heart skips a beat

Solid ground beneath

Reality is a beast

Thunder roars ahead

Gnat flies in circles

An annoying distraction

Causes quite a stir

Fresh air and water

Loved by family and friends

Life's purest pleasures

Words flowing freely

Gift of creativity

Blank canvas now full

Steppin'

I step into a room as if
the red soles of these
got-it-from-my-mama shoes
reveal riveting tales
of resilience…
because they do

I've been through some things
wearing my wish-I-hadn't-done-that shoes
You know, the ones we wear into the ground
wishing we could switch into some
comfortable running shoes
for the really hard lessons

I exhausted my bad-attitude shoes
I mean the toxic I-don't-give-a-Croc pumps
Pumped up to no-good
not long before I understood—
that path
was not paved
with good intentions

When trials appear
I cling to hope that centers me
I polish my wish-upon-a-star shoes
The ones with the sling backs and toes
pointing me in the right direction
I get serious… I pray

I revel in grace
dust myself off
put on my bring-home-the-bacon shoes
The sure-footed ones
with the sturdy heel
I step into my purpose
and don't look back!

Zaneta Varnado Johns is an internationally recognized poet and author of *Poetic Forecast, After the Rainbow, What Matters Journal* and *Encore*. She has co-authored collaborative books and co-edited two poetry anthologies. Johns was nominated for a Pushcart Prize in poetry. Her expressions appear in numerous literary publications. Colorado, USA

ZanExpressions.com

Cody Jones

Therapy

I've been running my whole life.

Excitement from play would fuel my feet to run towards my imagination. Towards my dreams of playing in front of crowds.

Skinny mixed-boy with a big head.

Racing my siblings and cousins from tree to tree.

Swinging my fists from hip to ear, lifting my knees I felt I could fly. First to touch the tree wins.

From there the race continues to the parking lot and back. Slower than them I was falling back.

Lighter than them, not fully Black.

No food for my stomach, no food for thought. Filled with anger I cried when I fought.

Bawling my eyes out while I bullied. Taking without asking.

I had nothing, so while they were in the classroom reading, I was in the hallways stealing. Grasping handfuls of change hoping it would change the feeling in the pit of my stomach. I learned about the haves and have-nots, not from class, but from the world.

Unprotected by the walls built by a system, and so I entered. Ripped and uprooted by police officers and awarded to my Mother. What did she win, and how did I aid her victory over my Father?

A battle over custody of my flesh.

A Tillamook Judge, I'll never forget those white stone steps. Running and searching for my siblings and cousins left behind.

I would run from corner to corner, not knowing what I would find.

I'm Cody Jones, and I was born and raised in Oregon then moved to the island of Kauai in 2019. My poetry path started as a youth going to therapy and journaling. I write about my experiences with the hopes that they bring empathy and solace to those who read my poems.

Jill Sharon Kimmelman

We

Slipping beneath waves of
silken turquoise waters

Our kisses, scented of ripe peaches,
forever remind me of summers with you

Peonies and poppies catch the summer wind
tickling noses,

our grand passion sealed in these moments

Until today 'twas you and me
from this moment on, it's forever we.

Jill Sharon Kimmelman is a two-time Pushcart Prize-nominee in Poetry.
Her international publishing credits include *Vita Brevis Press, Spillwords Press, Fine Lines, Better Than Starbucks Poetry & Fiction Journal, Poetic Musings, The Poet Magazine, ILA Magazine, Prolific Pulse Press LLC, World Inkers Network, Garden of Neuro, Writing In A Woman s Voice, PLCS, Eric Publications, and Prolific Pulsations.*

Teresa H. Klepac

Grass Dance for Old Lovers

When you sing, *Here comes the Sun,*
you dance in the grass as it struggles
to push forth green shoots. The spring in
your step brings sudden delight. Some
roll their eyes and cast a cock-eyed
look your way. With a grin, I sashay next to you,
kiss your neck and hug you until you laugh.
A good hug is worth a thousand
sighs of longing, a belly laugh twice as much.

When you sing, we lift our flabby
arms and shake our big booties
with abandon. We squeeze together
so we breathe each other's breath.
There are sparks in the air and in our eyes.

The delirious joy of living in a moment
is as sleek as the neighbor's goldendoodle
lounging on the rough porch.
Doesn't make much sense. Not that it has to.

The dog doesn't know what's got into us.
Love never gets old. Let's drink life's lemonade,
one squeeze at a time. Intertwined, let's savor
the denouement of winter's crusty, white grip.

Summer Sunburn

That transformative journey I packed for...
I forgot my toothbrush and a clean pair
of underpants. Traveling light is such a
delight. Consider it all joy, to step onto a
beach and know that your transformation
is at last in reach. With pictures of you
wearing white, with a blue sky and sand,
you're buff and sleek, with a glorious tan.
So much better than what you planned.
When the gulls fly squawking across
the horizon, you know you've found
the best kind of ground so sink in your toes
and right under your nose build a castle
out of the grainy beach and let the juice
from a fresh peach drip and soothe your
summer sunned lip while you bake until
you're lobster bright and you know that
the transformation is just about right. Ouch!

Autumn Joy

Skipping today

through leaves and sunlight on asphalt

Skipping today

move on, no cares, in autumn play.

Yellow, red flutters -- I won't halt

I can't be bothered, not my fault.

Skipping today.

Teresa H. Klepac, Columbia, MO.. is published in Still Points Arts Quarterly, Of Rust and Glass, TigerShark, Blood and Bourbon, and Pure Slush. She received honorable mention in MSPS poetry contests 2023/2022, PRA contest 2023, 3rd place in MSPS Contest 2022. She is writing a fantasy novel spiced with poetry.

Barbara Harris Leonhard

Gold

Caches of memories, the hidden biography of our lives.
Are we present to tears falling into streams of silence?
Do we hear the heart pulsing each shallow breath?
Do we notice the taste of ice? The sound of a leaf
screaming when wrenched from a branch by autumn wind?

The songs of hunger from a swan in a wetland pond?
The sting of sorrow burning the tongue and throat?

Our eyes sparkle, fireflies born to blaze
yet dimming into a flicker. Our glorious moments lapse
into a drowsy forever, or a haze on hope's horizon.
We cling to invisible kisses and lost shadows.
The lips sing hymns then wail laments.
How we sleep unlit, not seeking the hidden treasure
of the forever mundane lingering in our thirsty souls.

Barbara Harris Leonhard, a retired ESL instructor, has written a poetry collection *Three-Penny Memories: A Poetic Memoir* (Experiments in Fiction, 2022), which is about her relationship with her mother, who suffered from Alzheimer's. Barbara is also the Editor for MasticadoresUSA. She lives in Mid-Missouri with her husband and cat Jasper.

Donna McKinney

My Two Grandfathers

I spring from two lines, soil and salt water.

Merging together in a river of family bubbling
forth with children, grandchildren, great-
grandchildren.

One man tilled the Virginia soil,
planted seeds, harvested crops, lofted prayers,
and tended rainbows for his children.

The other man sailed bay waters,
ingathering the bounty of dancing crabs and fish,
a life measured out by trotlines, nets and
saltwater tides.

Families are like that. Not one thing. Or the other
thing.

But all the things.
Melded.
Soil and salt water.

Converging to make me who I am today.
Neither a farmer, nor a waterman.
But shaken, stirred, blended, a measure of the two.

I am soil. I am salt water.

We are all stardust.

Donna McKinney is a writer, mom, and nana to four grandchildren. For a long while she wrote about science and technology for the U.S. Navy. These days she writes kids' books, poems, and grocery lists. She lives in North Carolina with two delinquent hound dogs.

Danielle Martin

Capturing Happiness

Panning neither left nor right,
zooming into focus to capture
to bottle, to store, to savour

for when I'm too far away
to embrace, to feel,
to breathe, to absorb

through wandering cracks
when I'm falling apart
from the inside out
this magic that ignites my smile,
when no one looks.

What is this spell that speaks?

The very act of moving into something, yet to be.

The Soca tune that makes me cry, "Oh Gosh!"

The way my man, "knows"
the aching silence riding along like a dementor,
can easily be vanquished with great food,
like the carefully selected and purchased
creamy, cloudlike, potato salad and chicken pelau
well-seasoned, moist, peppered, exactly right,
making me go, "Hmmm," as I put the heaped,
plastic fork into his mouth and then mine.
And when all done, the way he rests his open palm,
flat on my stomach, saying, "Everything is alright."
A mantra that seeps into my subconscious
hopefully spilling and soaking into our futures.

The spell is surreal.

The warm night breeze swirling through my hair,
white ruffles running upon darkened shores,
the gentle, yet strong roar of the liquid beast
a warning and summons all at once.
A wooden tower, my reclaimed kingdom
surpassing the tops of glistening coconut trees.

It's the sip of the canned beer,
inching down my throat
quenching a thirst, I did not have,
pulsing a latent, vibrant, truer version of me out.

It is the non-verbal understanding and puzzle
between us.

It is the brisk downpour,
brushing against my face
urging raw acceptance of my fate.

It is newfound conversation.
The unexpected exchange of thought and
experiences.
A rekindling of my love for humanity
showing me that though we project
differently,
that, we are each other, after- all.

It is the teasing sleep that makes eyelashes meet.
The sight of my offspring coming to greet.
The bed that catches my morphing body
and the dreams that whisper sweet nothings into
me
charming me, slowly, tenderly,
into believing this magic is real
like a talisman it protects
as sounds of my journey carry,
about the room, all the way to the moon
until parrots shoot through candy skies,
shrill cries, causing me to rise.

Danielle Martin is a former Caribbean Journalist and Copywriter who seeks to add the title of poet to her name. Danielle's work appears in several international print and online anthologies. Additionally, her own poetry collection, "Kissing Shadows: Caribbean Love Poems," is available on Amazon. Find her on FB @DanielleM

Karuna Mistry

Judgement

Prepare.
Rejected.
Rejected.
Rejected…
And rejected.
Another reject.
Again, rejected.
One more reject.
Three more rejects.
Another dozen rejects.
Is there something wrong with me?
How long can I go on being rejected…?
  Dejected.
  Ejected.
Rejected… Rejected… Rejected…
Rejected. Rejected.
Rejected…
  Accepted.
  What…?
My work has been accepted!
Finally! Published! Glory!
Share the limelight!

Read. Rejoice!
Read again!
Real joy!

Prepare another submission.
This is a new trend -
Sigh, rejected.
And repeat.
Rejected...

Youniversal Contemplation (being and to be)

my father whom i once knew
we exchanged love, long ago
on a blue tune, many moons

sit upon his empty seat
custodian yellow throne
lord over what i can see

journey of a lost star
distant white lotus love
he reaches from afar

nothing can be further
black stellar creation
a child and a father:

journey of yourself
your only journey
just open yourself
yell out Jehovah.

from morn to set
i meditate
his qualities
i contemplate

Allah, Krishna
Rama, Vishnu
Waheguru
Yahweh…

until i unite
in delight
and **joy**

Incarnations, Incantations and Carnations

Two dozen avatar incarnations spread their divine
Appearances on the lunar-solar combined calendar
Dates of demi-gods, semi-gods, saints and gurus
The devotee spoilt for choice on birthdays to celebrate
Apparently, some are famous but others go unnoticed
Not that the supreme personality of Godhead minds
For They are undisturbed, aloof and wholly unattached
To the freewill of the wise, but often folly, human race

Bring flowers of carnations, fruits, greens or water
Offer them with one's love and They will accept
The House of God is a lively, colourful, busy place
Of entrance bells, instruments, books and plates

Chant holy incantations that are, by nature,
Enchanting by their repetitive aural flavour
Which invoke attraction of the attracted
To the supreme attractor - as bees to nectar

Devotional taste is never quite the same
Anywhere - at home, in a car, train or plane
For seven days without God makes one weak

Hear, sing, play, paint, draw, write, clean,
Worship, meditate, serve and eventually
Learn to make friends with the Supreme

A brief moment of perfect bliss is all one needs
To pave the path of perfection to the Lord
Irrespective of material qualification and birth
It is our intrinsic nature, our inner dharma
The doer cannot be separated from their act

What gives me deep joy is seeing that Monsoon Boy
By way of reciprocation in the temple of my heart

In the space of two years, Karuna Mistry has published over 60 poems in more than 40 anthologies covering life, music, science fiction and spirituality. His creativity includes magazine editorship, photography, drawing and blogging. Karuna co-authors his debut poetry book with his sister, Pratibha Savani.

https://www.instagram.com/karunamistrypoetry/

https://karunacreations.wordpress.com/

Howard Moon

Unrelated incidents

Joy like life is not a single momentary event
It is a continuum of happenings
Strung together
Often by unrelated
Seemingly insignificant occurrences
Beyond our control and comprehension

Hidden happiness

Happiness hides itself well
Cloaked in mystery and even pain
Waiting for just the right moment
To jump out
And shout
Gotchu
Followed by peals of cascading laughter

Howard Moon is a writer and poet. His writing and poetry have appeared in multiple collections and anthologies, Small Change, Montana Mouthful, Das Literarisch Journal, Of Poets and Poetry, Native Skin, Breath and Shadow, Ariel Chart, and more. He is of Native heritage and identifies as BIPOC. He is a brain injury survivor and suffers from mental illness. He lives in central Florida.

Michelle Ayon Navajas

Rainbow - Colored Afternoon

rainbow - colored afternoon sky
people dancing just to get by
children laughing, popcorn on the side
moms smiling, dreams amplified
dads hoping, brighter future they eye.

crossword puzzle and scrabble to try
little kid, a word to describe whining and sigh
with dad on the lookout by her side
rainbow - colored afternoon...

many years and many moons gone by
memories linger, at times with teary eye
with dreams coming true, it takes pride
all the love in the world to coincide
missing a loved one beside, tears to cry
rainbow - colored afternoon...

Blessing

if this isn't a blessing, then i don't know what to call this
the birds that keep on singing amidst the chilly morning rain
the luscious green meadows that never cease to thrive come rain or shine.

if this isn't an absolute grace, then i don't know what to call this
the dusk diminishes the night, paving the way
for the sun that never fails to promise a better morning
and a restful sunset.

if this isn't luck, then i don't know what to call this
the life so good dripping with smiling friends around
random people oozing with compassion
neighbors who hate less and love more.

so get up and smile, for life is not bad at all
you alone mean the whole world to me.

I Didn't Know

Beauty

i didn't know leaves could dance gracefully
as the wind blows upon the signal of the monsoon rain
while it pitter-patters on the roof
i didn't know loud rumbling thunder could sound
like a love song; so gentle and so sweet
i didn't know a tremendous flash of lightning could look
like fireworks at night, flashing spectacular lights in jubilant celebration
i didn't see the beauty in them until the day i found you
i didn't know beauty as much as I knew it when i had you.

Butterflies

i didn't know butterflies ever lived inside me
waiting to fly, waiting to soar
until the day i saw you, i felt fluttering sensations
as if a million little butterflies were screaming, wanting to be freed

every single cell in my body was churning,
cramping,
feeling anxious, shaking, shivering, twitching by
just the sight of you,
i didn't know butterflies could live in my stomach
until i saw you
i didn't know butterflies could go crazy, as crazy
as they became when i had you.

Burned

i didn't know love could be magical and enchanting
and bewitching, until the day you took my hand by
the door, gently
caressing my hair, your eyes
with a loving steady gaze, and then slowly you
moved closer to me,
i felt the warmth of your body, the tenderness of
your lips,
the fire in your heart giving me burning sensations
then i was burned, burned down to ashes by your
touch,
by your embrace, by your kiss
i didn't know i could get burned by love until
i was burned, burned by your love.

Michelle is a Filipino International Bestselling author, published 9 poetry books and 1 flash fiction book. Five of her 10 books are #1Amazon Bestselling books.

Nimitok

Cooked

Loyalty calls, within the azure fire's embrace,
Tending meat to perfection, in its fiery place.
Unbeknownst, the pot betrays with venison's broth's escape,
Offering itself to the flames, a subtle twist of fate.

Steaming burnt aromas rise from the earthen pot's crack,
The mind envisions the contents, hues in the memory stack.
Chalky, the residue left in edible charcoal's track,
An active nutrient transformed, a culinary hijack.

The Ambassador

That single light amidst the gloom
Called a ward off the doom
Master of the blind; the one-eyed
Motions to the lost, protects the led
Although nostalgia draws his thought
The ambassador must home come naught

Chosen from the multitude of best
Joined to the journey of eternal bliss
Ravished by the thought of the awaited glory
Sought continuously for means to remain first
Rewarded with the chains of gore

Mounted on by the horse of shadows
Example laid, much be to the glory of Cardow
Forget the life of freedom; live for the people
Amply treading on the red carpet; no thorns imbedded
Forgiveness for everyone's sin.

The Dancer's Rhythm

Arms outstretched, from west to east,
Head bowed with a painful grin, this lad's release,
Thighs parting gently, toes tap the ground,
Chest rises swiftly, a hunter's rebound,
Striking with a warrior's grace, then pausing to
breathe.

Evoke the leaves' rhythm, in the wind they sway,
The masquerade emerges, in dance's display,
The dancer's spirit connects with voices unheard,
Concealing tales of heroes, with crossed feet interred,
Seducing the earth like a drunken escapade.

Oh, breeze, sway through mortality's gate,
Evoke immortality, the dance can't abate,
Stop, walk, tiptoe, crawl, and then start,
The beaded waist, moves with a rhythmic heart,
Writhing like a broken doll, emerging bold and great,
The dancer knows its spirituality, a cleansing rite's
weight.

Tolu Adeniyi (Nimitok) is a young creative whose literary exposure although harnessed by her degree in English and Literary studies, is a result of her view of life. Words and its intended and its contextual experiences drives her poetic expression. As a child she enjoys folklores, takes by moonlight, woke soyinka, Clark people, and others, who gave premises to her literature exposure and exploration. Someday she believes African Literature will influence the world's culture.

Gypsie-Ami Offenbacher-Ferris

Angel Wings

Angel wings flutter by
on the backs of butterflies
Translucent as the sky is blue
dappled sunlight shining through

A flash of light in the night
the snap of a batwing in flight
His wings are of blackest black
a furtive glance to watch them flap

Stray pieces of rainbow-colored hues
caught in the flow of summer's perfuse
Hummingbird's bounce limb to limb
their own private troponym

Angels all are not in heaven
many are here in their earthen haven
No matter the color of wings or skin
angels all we have within

The Walkway

There is a walkway in my mind,
I travel through it
from time to time.

My breathing slows,
I cross my legs
and travel far below.

Along the tree-lined
path I find several old
friends of mine.

Waiting patiently near
the bank my beautiful
timber wolf appears.

Flying strongly overhead
her wings outstretched
the hawk in sky does tread.

Into the trees I now spy
a massive buck
his rack so high.

Then through the water
crystal clear a sweet
blue dolphin brings up the rear.

All are guides my friends
it's true they come to me
my heart does mend.

Dolphin's Song

I want to sing the dolphin's song
as we swim gently along
Riding the wondrous Gulf Stream
deliciously warm and azure blue -
Wouldn't you?

I long to be a part of their pod
feel their heartbeats so strong
Fin to fin as we traverse the sea
all and all in complete harmony -
With me.

So happy to be immersed every day
gliding whichever way
The tides decide our traveling fate
jump up and down flop to and fro -
Let's go!

I'd play in the frothy white caps
flip up high land on my back
Dive as deep as I could
shoot up high once again -

Happy grin.

At end of day when dark as night
water and sky merge in sweet delight
Within my pod of dolphin kind
I'd close my eyes and rest my mind -
No thought of humankind.

Gypsie-Ami Offenbacher-Ferris lives in Southport, NC. Published in *Whisper's & Echoes*, *50 Give or Take*, *Visual Verse*, *Spillwords*, and in *Wounds I Healed*. Honorable Mentioned in *Tales from the Moonlit Path 2021 Halloween Challenge*. Gypsie-Ami has recently completed a chapbook merging her poetry and photography titled *Reflections of a Woman's Life*.

Thomas King Oloo (Babs)

Let Me Rise

Let me rise even when I fall
Let me sit atop
The tree that gives
Let me swim in the depths
Of untold fulfilment
And ride with the ride of a great ride
Let me rise, let me rise

Do you know?
I am the girl that lives
In the world of a dream
And dreams of great things
I am the girl that wears
The crown of a jerrican
And carry water home
To a waiting lot unknowingly irate
Let me rise above this crown, let me rise

I walk the market
And walk the roads home
My crown; the basket of unsold wheat
My bangles; lucky coins from my trade
I walk lost in my dream
For a moment my dream gives me refuge
Oh! Let me rise.

Thomas King Oloo is a Kenyan, born and raised in the lakeside city of Kisumu. He is a teacher of English Language and Literature in English. He is passionate about writing poems as well as stories. He finds great pleasure in reading the poems of Edgar Allan Poe, Ezra Pound and Emilly Dickinson.

K. Ann Pennington

My Moon and Stars

He is the moon and she is the stars.
A moody moon who loves from afar.
Stars—I've seen more in the West;
viewed from Maine woods are the stars I like best.

Stubborn and insolent, shoots first then asks.
Every moment has its tasks.
Hides true feelings.
Shouts them aloud.
Peeks from under Saturn's rings.
Rides atop the clouds.

But temperamental changes tune;
from crescent to half to complete la lune.
When the last of twelve talks—
a hawk walks the walk.

That wild child of the zodiac
leads other stars across moon's path.
Closer they get in nighttime's sky,
they band together and fight sun's eye.

Same safe harbor from a different approach.
Knowing full well neither's above reproach, for some never know
the love moon and stars broach.

But trying, still, to find a way
to reach me now from far away.
To shine their lights from there to here,
and let me feel as if they're near.

My guiding lights—
my moon and stars,
please never leave me, wherever we are.

K Ann Pennington is fascinated by the constructed nature of place and has traveled over 30,000 miles studying America. She focuses specifically on primary source materials and performing field research on a variety of topics, especially the Civil War. More about K Ann's stories can be found at https://kannpennington.wordpress.com/

Dawn Pisturino

The Phoenix

I rose out of the ashes and spread my wings,
A phoenix forced to look at the world with
different eyes.
Green was greener and blue was bluer,
Deep and rich and vibrant as life itself.
The yellow sun warmed me with his brilliant rays,
Held me in his arms,
And caressed my downy feathers
With a newborn father's pride.
Suddenly, he flung me into the air,
Forcing me to flap my wings and fly.
Wind held me up and steered me west.
Misty clouds passed me by.
I was free again!
No residual guilt and shame from my previous life.
No destructive attachments to weigh me down.

No more smiling faces backstabbing me in the dark.

My heart was clean; my soul was pure.

Rebirth! Resurrection! Rejuvenation and Life!

What joy I felt in this newfound spring.

I landed on a distant shore -

On a tiny island - and began to live again.

The Window

The old woman sits by a cracked window,
Gazing out over the past
And a lonely road, straight and narrow,
Running past the house.
Weeds, curled and brown,
Grow up through the broken pavement.
Barren trees, bent by winter winds,
Bow their heads to a few passing cars.
She cocks her head, listening for the sound
Of an old pickup truck.
That was you, Dad,
Driving slowly down the road to the house
Where your lady love stood waiting
By the side of the road so many years ago.
She still remembers the hands that
Waved at her and honked the horn,
And the smile that flashed,
Signaling your affection for her.

Her dull blue eyes brighten,

Her lips curl into a smile,

And a cry of joy escapes that puckered mouth

As she waves from the window at your lingering ghost.

Waking Up the Corpse

You made me
feel
the rich colors and music
of life
the joy and sorrow
and all the notes in between.
I blessed you and cursed you
for waking up the corpse.
It was so easy
to walk around
empty and dead inside.
Knife-twisting emotion
keeps me up
turns on the tears
brings me down
pushes me to the heights
of raw ecstasy.
I need you
and thank you
for making me feel again.

Dawn Pisturino is a retired nurse in Arizona whose publishing credits include poems, short stories, and articles. Her poetry has appeared in several anthologies, most recently in *Hidden in Childhood: A Poetry Anthology*, *Wounds I Healed: The Poetry of Strong Women*, and the *2023 Arizona Literary Magazine*.

Sarah Merritt Ryan

Just Dance

Here I am

My son and I

On the dance floor

All eyes on just us.

Old pop song plays

One that I love

My boy asks

Dance with me mommy!

Do I dance? Should I dance?

Finally letting go

Dancing like at home

Only my toddler sees.

Why should I not

And so I do

I watch his moves

His passion for it.

I set myself free
Dancing around him
I let go and move
No thinking just feeling.

I move my body and arms
Losing myself in the beat
Feeling like my true self
Achieving victory.

For freedom I celebrate
Remission from illness
Thrill for becoming a mother
Pride in forgetting myself.

Stepping and turning
Twirling around my little one
Moving as he likes
When we dance at home.

My son is my reason

Dancing with him

An exclamation point

On hard-earned recovery.

My past over

Think little of future

Just appreciate existing

Feeling alive.

Joy is letting go

Not asking for anything more

Than the day we've been given

Making every moment count.

Sarah Merritt Ryan is a poet, blogger, and writer of memoir. She writes of her experiences with emotionally surviving serious mental illness, telling her unique story. Her poetry has been published in anthologies by Whispering Angels Books, Prolific Pulse Press, PurpleStone Press, and Garden of Neuro Institute.

Pratibha Savani

Delightful Moods

(Imagine)

~ Red

A giant streak glosses across the page

(Estimate)

~ Orange

Vigorous swirls dance in the soaring heat

(Analyse)

~ Yellow

Vibrant splashes burn the atmosphere

(Reflect)

~ Green

Dynamic strokes breathe new life

(Smile)

~ Blue

Waves of coolness cascades beneath

(Grin)

~ Purple

Soothing shades paint the perfect colour night

Breath of Joy

Stretching up. Touch the sky (Urdhva Hastasana)

Hello world!! Sun Salutations begins (Surya Namaskar)

Breathe....

Stretching down. Forward Fold (Uttanasana)

Let's plank. Hold 1 2 3....Breathe....

Steadily I slide into Knees, Chest, Chin

(Ashtanga Namaskara)....Breathe....

Gently moving up into the Cobra....Yes!....Breathe....

Griping into Downward Facing Dog

(Adho Mukha Svanasana). Holding....Woof!....Breathe....

Back to Forward Fold. Stretching up

One round complete. Phew!....Breathe....

Round two. Here I go....Breathe....

~ ~ ~ ~ ~ ~ ~ ~

I am the Warrior One (Virabharasana I)

Hips flexed....Thighs holding strong....Yes!...Breathe....

Continuing into the Warrior Two (Virabhadrasana II)

Arms balanced....Just a bit further!....Breathe....

Stretching up with the Triangle Twist (Trikonasana)

Just a little bit more!....Breathe....

Straightening up. My hands are raised (Urdhva Hastasana)

Formed into a magnificent tree (Vrksasana)....Breathe....

~ ~ ~ ~ ~ ~ ~ ~

Sitting down. The soles meet.

At ease in Cobbler's Pose (Baddha Konasana)....Breathe....

Slowly loosening down (Savasana)....Muscles relax ♡

Staying here a little while longer....Breathe....

Final cooldown!!

In blissful Baby Pose (Ananda Balasana)

Stretch in relief....Breathe!....

Sinking into the Child's Pose (Balasana)

Muscles unwind....Aaahhh....Final Breaths!

And Breathe.

Pratibha Savani is a UK poet, artist and author of 'Tangles + Knots'. Published in over forty-five literary publications including anthologies, she is a creative soul, inspired by the cosmos, nature and spirituality. Pratibha likes to defy the rules with her inventive expressions on instagram and facebook as @pratibhapoetryart.

Shiela Denise Scott

Loyal Love

Loyalty, you reside in me,
From the time you were planted,
As a mustard seed,
Faith, you shined through,
Times of dim lit exposure,
With no point of view,
Promise, you fulfilled the times,
No one assumed you'd come true,
Honest, you have remained,
And in love, you pushed through,
Difficulties, no one assumed would happen,
But they did,
Override sadness with happiness,
And overcame the jest of tears,
Fears, that could no longer belong,
Shivers stood still,
Awakened by the improvisions,
Of believing in his joyful tiers,
That self could now uplift alone.

Conversation with a Friend

Familiar sounds of a long-lost echo,

That resounded in my dreams,

Awakened to the thought of her,

Succumb to reality,

Calls on the phone ring,

Text messages come clear,

Instagram notifications,

That can't be deleted,

Nor feared,

Love found in the moment,

Of emotional similarity,

Once the voice of silence,

Was heard,

from a friendly being.

Music

Sounds of tomorrow,

Recorded today,

Laughter of the moment,

Remembered in a psalms delay,

Of verses in motion,

Chorus on display,

The purpose of a song in heart,

Expressing itself upon the face,

Of many.

Shiela Denise Scott, creative with an earned Bachelor of Fine Arts Degree in Creative Writing from Full Sail University, and a digital photography Associate of Arts and Science from Antonelli college, was awarded a light award for a Letter. Her poetry skills are displayed in multiple anthologies and journals.

Richa Dinesh Sharma

Chai and Sugar

Some Chai meetings are just too special

the tea is generously laced with a sisterly concern

a friendly spice boiled with cinnamon,

its flavour a tad stronger than ginger

The mugs are huge, different sizes and designs

one has Winnie the pooh and the other Tigger and such

remnants of a full nest, now comfort in an empty one

This is a 'treat' with store bought fried goodies

fluffy sponge cake and potato filled puff pastries

There's sobbing even when there's palpable joy

a pair of eyes watches the other for signs of pain

telling them to celebrate this huge 'milestone',

children growing into successful young adults,

chicks taking their first flight in the skies of their dreams

This empty nest keeps calling to all mother birds

like a beacon of shared heartache and endless cups of chai

words are redundant as gratitude is passed in hugs

the steady palm of one hand

reassures the tremors of a worried one

hands are held, banal jokes exchanged

It is a celebration indeed, everyone says,

to the enduring, fueling spirit of motherhood everywhere

And sugar is mixed just before everyone lifts their cups

Celebrating Love

Age-old February tradition, a month of Love
such a grand euphemism for human affection
fondness, affliction, enamour, lust even
scaling down a whole spectrum of feelings
like a rainbow stuck inside a prism
the magic our mind celebrates each day
with a visceral rhythm that changes every time
and the musics of all love songs ever written
igniting the emotional hyperdrive
and launching into a time-dilated eternity
of paradoxical bliss and hormonal roller-coasters
in time for the grandest fete of the human mind
A lifelong festival that outlives lives
Even as the hair greys and bones whittle down
they say, the hors d'oeuvres have just arrived

Mornings Are A Question...

...that I ask myself in a flurry of activities
as I push my children on and get them ready
to go and 'do their learning' while they still have minds
to go and dance while the music is blaring out
to play with friends all the games that are silly
to placate their teacher's loving ire with a smile
And, then when they're gone for the day,
I sip on my chai and look out the window,
listening to parakeets, sunbirds, and cuckoos
and looking at the greenest trees
I have a small revelry of my own,
a meditative rave party inside
I give loud, eccentric thanks to the Universe
for the miracles of friendship, love, and parenthood
for making magical people into my life
for making them say the healing words
for making them stay by my side

for mentors who did all the mentoring

and strangers who chose to believe in me

For my children it is a lesson early in life

that moments can be dressed over time

in well-thought colours of every joy,

their invisible faces painted as a core memory,

a continuously happy defiance

to the sanding and blunting edge of life

And when they ask me why

If not now, then when

is a question with which I reply

Richa Dinesh Sharma lives in Singapore with her husband, two human children and one furchild. Her poems have featured in *FineLines* quarterly issues, *OpenDoor Poetry* magazine, *MockingHeart Review*, *Medium* and several anthologies. She dabbles in Art when not writing or daydreaming. On Instagram @dryink_brush, email: richa.soul@gmail.com

Nicole Smith

Ordinary Joy

People overlook simple joy,
it's all around.
Yet we become numb to
ordinary instances of
peace and happiness
that simply exist.
The smell of coffee brewing,
the changing of seasons,
laughter, in all forms,
a song that evokes nostalgia,
falling in love,
a soft blanket on a chilly day.
There is joy all around
if only we'd open our eyes.

Chaos vs Joy

I grew up with Chaos-
he'd barge in screaming,
slamming cupboards, punching walls,
unexplainably breaking down.
He'd storm out in a fury,
stay away, allowing a false sense of calm
to tiptoe into the house until I was lulled
into a false sense of security.
He'd return to tear down any semblance
of stability I managed to cobble together.
Joy is peace.
Joy is quiet.
Joy is safety, stability, and security.
Joy is never angry.
Joy is a state of knowing
I am okay, I'll be okay,
and that Chaos
will never have a key
to the home full of Joy
I created for myself.

Joy is seeing two people hopelessly in love come together to celebrate.

It is also your friend finally breaking up with that narcissist,

knowing her heart is sad now, but that she dodged a terrible fate.

Joy is getting good news, you thought may never come.

It is also when your cousin's football team doesn't make the playoffs,

after endlessly listening to him expound on why his team is #1.

Joy is a surprise gift arriving at your door.

It is also setting boundaries with your "ism" filled aunt

And her angrily explaining that she will not bother coming anymore.

Joy is seeing a rainbow after a rough day.

It is also finally realizing your worth is not connected

To how much you weigh.

Joy is all around, in big ways and in small

If you train yourself to see it,

You'll be happier overall.

Nicole Smith is an advocate for mental health and body acceptance. She lives just outside of Pittsburgh with her husband and daughters. If Nicole isn't writing poetry, you can find her with her nose in a book.

Ivor Steven

Flowers in the Sky

Look up high
Beyond yesterday's goodbyes
Until your eyes
Are caressed by the sunny sky
And savor the reason why
Flowers strive to fly

That's What Friends Are For

"Help!" yelled Billy the Bee
Who was stuck, knee-deep
In the storm's fallen debris
"I'll be there as quick as
my body can shuffle along"
Said Charlie the concerned caterpillar

"My tiny toes are trapped
and I cannot fly free" Burbled Billy
Charlie sways and cleverly uses his snout
To nudge the broken twigs aside
And in a jiffy
Billy was able to wriggle free

A relieved Billy
Blessedly buzzes over Charlie
"Thank you kindly
for your gracious help
my dear friend"
"That's what friends are for"
Cheered Charlie the caterpillar

Ivor Steven was formerly an Industrial Chemist, then a Plumber, now retired, He has had numerous poems published in anthologies, and on-line magazines. He has 2 self-published books, "Tullawalla" and "Perceptions," and is a member of the Geelong Writers Inc. (Australia), and an appointed writer for "Coffee House Writers" magazine (USA

Gabriel S. Weah

My Vow

Cocoa of my complexion,

And dream of my sleep,

You're my perfect variation.

Your smiles danced in my heart.

The image captures my mind.

When you speak, the world sticks.

When you walk, the world freezes.

My happiness is in you.

And without you, my voice will perish.

You're truly loving and supportive.

On your lips, I've found my happiness.

You're my dream junction.

Tonight, please, you must be my vow.

I love you, sweet dream.

And without you, my light will go off.

Poet, essayist, life coach and mentor, teacher (by profession), and devout Christian, Gabriel S. Weah, alias "Lyrical Genius," is an eminently multi-talented Liberian award-winning poet who learned his writing career in a dream. Lyrical Genius, as he is commonly called, hails from Sinoe County, Liberia, and was born unto the federation of Mr. and Mrs. Weah.

Lynn White

And Then

Stand up!
Stand out
from the crowd
of follow my leaders.
Dance in the rain
sing out of tune
unfurling
your red umbrella.

Wear red in the dark
to be seen.
And then,
it's your scene.
And then,
all is possible
then.

Holding The Sunlight

She learned to catch the sunlight
to hold it in her hands
and let it warm them
with the scents of summer
to let its rays shine through
then open her fingers wide
and let it go free.

Towards The Light

We always headed for the light
like the forest trees
we wanted
to leave the darkness behind
and push ourselves up
tall and straight
unwavering.
Now you're following us
making a new pathway
through.
And when you see
the red worms of sunlight
seeking you out
and penetrating you
as they pass through.
you will know.
You will know
you've reached
your destination.
These worms won't devour you though,
they'll let you through
to where you were meant to be.

Lynn White lives in north Wales. Her work is influenced by issues of social justice and events, places and people she has known or imagined. She is especially interested in exploring the boundaries of dream, fantasy and reality. https://lynnwhitepoetry.blogspot.com and https://www.facebook.com/Lynn-White-Poetry-1603675983213077/

Charlotte Alexandria Williams

Golden Grandeur

Untrodden were the surfaces that lay beneath our feet
Where mountain tops and rivers stirred relentlessly to meet
A normal day upon this earth two billion years ago
Would soon be metamorphic rock and igneous below

With layers quilted over time defining what will be
The inner gorge eroded sculpting art in history
An action of tectonic plates was shifted at the core
Immovable this structure carving beauty on its floor

Before the print of man the waters ran so far and wide
With horizontal symmetry as earth and skies collide
An overflow of ebb and tow with secret avenue
Shall pave a way for life to stay in Arizona view

The isostatic force shall ever lift this amber gold
For nature is the entity we stunningly behold
With valleys steep that interchange and narrowly apply
An effortless creation manifests the human eye

A canyon stands from this day forth still widening its crate
With crystalline burnt at the root of undetermined fate
And miles below are streams that weave with gradient decrease
For California is the home that shields a masterpiece

Oak

Beneath the highs of wanton skies a ruling majesty
builds agriculture in our hearts supporting history
With luscious leaves his hardy sleeves provident of a home
that root in all significance and life to freely roam

Deciduous and dominant in woodlands widely spread
with pinkish browns the blossoming rejuvenating dead
A sprightly sight compels the light with warmth and sweet caress
And alternate unevenly through seasonal distress

A hemisphere that's evergreen extending latitude
Shall flourish universally with temperance to mood
Distinguished groups monoecious with heritage appeal
Shall guard with couplet geneses and naturalistic feel

When history resembles oak as merely just a tree
he'll rule the skies with gracefulness that sprout periphery
With luscious leaves his hardy sleeves may falter and combust
yet anchored is significance, and roots defined as trust.

Charlotte is a creative writer from Kent who started writing at the age of 21. Having dabbled in both prose and poetry she tends to touch upon topics involving mental health and grief in the hope she can help people to not feel so alone, plus inspire people to always try and find a light in the dark.

Lindsay Soberano Wilson

Glimmers

They say
you can turn triggers into glimmers
They say
you can pull the trigger or see the glitter
They say
you can turn that frown upside down
They say
you can pull yourself out of the dark

I say
I've been facing my triggers
only after digging out of the whirlwind
of disasters that formed into plaster
swirls on the ceilings of my heart and home

I say
I've been unearthing the triggers
suddenly, they aren't that much bigger
and I can step outside of me to see
Glimmers
reflect back at me
vibrating and humming like the
Shimmering Northern Lights.

Dancing Through the Dark

Dancing in the dark

Dancing through the dark

Dancing with the dark

Dancing out the dark.

Find Something You Love

"Find something you love"
I found myself saying to my 12-year-old

anything will do
just something
to put your mind to

and put everything
on the line for

and not give up on
not for anyone
(not even you.)

A craft that you can craft
where you don't need a map
but there's no looking back

Something to lose yourself in
and find yourself in

both at the same time.

Lindsay Soberano Wilson recently released her debut poetry collection *Hoods of Motherhood* (Prolific Pulse Press, 2023), a bittersweet reflection on becoming a mother. Her chapbook, *Casa de mi Corazón: A Travel Journal of Poetry and Memoir*, explores how her sense of community, Canadian Jewish identity, and home was shaped by travel. Her second poetry book *Breaking Up With the Cobalt Blues: Poems for Healing* (Prolific Pulse Press, 2024) is forthcoming.

Chanah Wizenberg

Cadence Lost, Cadence Found

Part 1

2020 COVID-19 changed the cadence
of life worldwide. Forcing us into
seclusion

It was a strange new life
Disrupting our metered cadence
without a proper coda
or any rhythm at all

Now for the first time
I had to stay home
Alone

All my life I was either at school, work,
ballet, or band. Seven days a week

The rhythms of my life perfectly synced
The order of each beat pre-set
providing structure for my ADHD brain

I'll never forget that ten-minute warning
before the CODA that would change all our lives
standing in the aquatic's office in our
swimsuits ready to teach lessons

The air squeezing out while we waited
Subdued silence filling the room
Icey tentacles of fear stabbed at
my heart as I looked from
face to face to face
of the college students.
What would this mean for them?

Lockdown ordered
Ten-minutes to
vacate
the building
COVID-19
was here

It's theme
PANDEMIC

Life as we knew it
was over. For how long
No one knew

I sat in my apartment,
staring at my dog and cat

They stared back clueless of
the sense of doom, fear, and
foreboding filling the room

What now?
My worst enemy has infiltrated
my life, unstructured time

There were YouTube videos
of folks making sourdough bread

Sour dough
there's a poem in there
Somewhere

It came to me then
I have time.
Time to write and mete
out a new rhythm

Create a new cadence
with a steady pulse,
a powerful beat
for this global
time out

Settling into a New Rhythm

Part 2

Upon waking to my cat pawing
my face and my dog blinking sleepy
eyes towards me, while thumping her tail
our morning rhythm begins

I dress, make the bed, feed the hungry
hound and the capricious cat

Breakfast done, it's time for "walkies"
Asha lumbers along beside me, her
overweight belly waddling side to side

Back home, time for treats and my
own breakfast of egg, toast, and coffee
While enjoying a second cup, I peruse
Facebook and email

When the coffee hits my bloodstream,
and my meal, is a warm comfort in my belly,
I'm ready to rock and roll

Sitting at my laptop, I open up
Scrivener and choose my novel project

Mornings are for writing
Afternoons are for swimming
maybe errands if I must
another walk for Asha girl

Evenings are for poetry, reading,
maybe watching TV, a British mystery
or Rachel Maddow, if today is Monday

I need music too
especially on cleaning day,
and working out; music
takes the pain away.

It took a while to find my way
I fought it for so long
COVID changed my life
as it did for all the people
around the whole wide world

Hey, did you know?
The world's an ouroboros
I never thought of that before

Anyway, I'm not the only one
who was made to change
A do or die kind of feeling
comes to mind
That was the perception
when the whole wide world shut down
Do or die
But I digress

I have found the rhythm of my life
a new cadence, breathing life in and out
A great big Tower* almost took me out,
as I don't do change so well

I need a little nudge
or an outright shove,
hence the Tower time
to find my place, my rhythm,
the true cadence of my life

How about you?
Did the global time out,
the big Tower moment
force you to find your path?

*The Tower is a reference to the Tower card in tarot. It represents forced massive change, upheaval, and destruction in order to birth a new beginning.

*Ouroboros: a circular symbol that depicts a snake or dragon devouring its own tail and that is used especially to represent the eternal cycle of destruction and rebirth. https://www.merriam-webster.com/dictionary/Ouroboros

Chanah Wizenberg's poems, stories, and articles have been published in several anthologies and magazines, including the Heron Clan, Vol 8, Reflections & Revelations, TAF Omnibus, Vol 2, Fines Lines, and Cary Magazine. She's a retired ballerina, pastry chef, and English teacher. In her free time Chanah swims and lifeguards at her local YMCA. She resides in Raleigh, North Carolina with her dog, Asha, and her cat, Marmalade.

Lisa Tomey-Zonneveld

Stars Wash Across the Sky

Stars wash across the sky, melt into the dark
Just the same, they watch over, always feel the spark
Never too small to be seen, underneath or deep below
Sowing down into the soil,
seedlings push their chance to grow
Smite upon the cabbages, cuts into potatoes
Onions cry from pulls so tight, legumes wax sharp blows
Winds blow rough into the grasses, toss the rains about
Suns comes up to foster growth, butters come to cups
Bush beans fill with seeds, so full,
ready for the next phase
Onions plump, those left behind,
for their winter storage place
Growth from under, growth from above,
showers wash over us
Never miss a single chance to serenade
dear nature's love
Aligned we go, aligned we grow,
aligned we prosper overflow
No matter what may come this way,
the mind will always know
It's a blaze of hope that warms the crops,
left to life to breathe
It's a chance at warmth and freshness full
that makes life ever be

I Have Found My People

A stop at the orthopedic clinic

I watch the walker, with a rollator cross the walkway

elders hobble, take a slower pace

as I reach a parking place

attach the handy-capable flag

awareness makes its rounds

as I push off slowly from my seat

and check my hair in the mirror

these are gentle reminders

I am one of the silver amblers

I have found my people

Lisa Tomey-Zonneveld is the founder/manager of Prolific Pulse Press LLC and a widely published poet and writer. She is an editor of numerous anthologies and for *Fine Lines Journal.* She is Poet Laureate Emeritus of Garden of Neuro Institute and is an organizer for Living Poetry in North Carolina. ProlificPulse.blog

Thank You

To Zaneta Varnado Johns for her excellence and dedication with editing and her encouragement for our anthologies and poetry.

To all the participants who have made this another beautiful anthology.

Prolific Pulse.Com

www.ingramcontent.com/pod-product-compliance
Lightning Source LLC
Chambersburg PA
CBHW030135010826
48973CB00002B/569

9781962374903